THE LAW OF CYCLES

THE LAW OF CYCLES

Finding Your Rhythmic Inner Peace

ELIZABETH CLARE PROPHET

SUMMIT UNIVERSITY PRESS®
Gardiner, Montana

THE LAW OF CYCLES
Finding Your Rhythmic Inner Peace
Elizabeth Clare Prophet

For information: The Summit Lighthouse,
63 Summit Way, Gardiner, MT 59030 USA.
1-800-245-5445 / 406-848-9500
TSLinfo@TSL.org
www.SummitLighthouse.org

Library of Congress Control Number: 2021938079
ISBN: 978-1-60988-367-6
ISBN: 978-1-60988-333-1 (eBook)

SUMMIT UNIVERSITY PRESS®

Disclaimer and Notes: (1) The violet flame and the information in this book are not intended to replace qualified advice of professionals licensed in the fields of physical and mental health, finance or law. No guarantee is made by Summit University Press that the practices or meditations described in this book will necessarily yield successful results. The practice and proof of the science of being rests with the individual. (2) We consider God to be both masculine and feminine and therefore refer to the Father-Mother God. However, we have sometimes referred to God as *he* or *him* for readability and simplicity in the text. (3) The stories in this book are true or are based upon true stories that were changed slightly to protect the privacy of the individuals.

24 23 22 21 1 2 3 4

CONTENTS

INTRODUCTION

THE PROCESSION OF LIFE

The galaxy is spinning out its spiral arms in space.

The cosmic magnet drives the heart of worlds—
fluids of life pulsating in a rhythmic ebb and flow.

Chromosomes align in precise array.
Behold the miracle of creation.

Gaze into the deep night sky and see the pulsar beating
in perfect time.

Drink the words of the poet as he sings
in perfect rhyme.

The electron in cyclic rhythm with the proton.

The planets in rhythm with the sun.
The solar system in rhythm with the galaxy.

Reverberations of the spheres in space echo
in the silence of our meditation.

There is harmony in God's creation!
There is rhythm. There is flow.

And cycles turn the wheels of time
as the Great Mother nurtures the procession of life.

Elizabeth Clare Prophet

- 1 -

SPIRALS OF CREATION

One of the great sources of comfort that has come to me in this life has been an understanding and a perception of the mathematical law and formula of the Law of Cycles whereby Spirit cycles through Matter and Matter cycles through Spirit.

We approach the Law of Cycles with reverence for the Creator whose Self-expression it contains. All evidence of its outworking in man, the earth, the elements, and the stars are but the tracings of his Being, footprints in the sands, tracks in the upper snows. Wherever we behold his markings as cyclings of infinity tumbling through the finite coils of time and space, there he has been. There his awful, wonderful Presence is—just beyond the veiled spirals of his creation.

Attempting to penetrate the Law of Cycles, we find secrets sublime and all-encompassing—the being of man the microcosm, in man the Macrocosm. These secrets have remained closely guarded by the adepts of the mystery schools for thousands of years, for an understanding of these laws provides a predictable platform of evolution—and the power to initiate cycles of our own.

KUTHUMI'S WORK ON CYCLES

The ascended master Kuthumi has influenced science and world thought for thousands of years. And it is he who has taught the Law of Cycles as fundamental to a comprehensive world view.

Embodied as the great master Pythagoras, Kuthumi expounded the law of the harmony of opposing forces. He taught how all of manifestation is composed of vibration in various states of interaction and equilibrium. We will see how this profound understanding is inherent in the cyclic law.

During the 1800s, Kuthumi—known to his Western students as Koot Hoomi Lal Singh, or K.H. —was an advanced adept. He had conquered the

The Ascended Master Kuthumi

usual ravages of time on the physical form, and it is said that for decades he continued to have the same youthful appearance. He was able to control the elements and to project a double of his physical body anywhere on the planet to perform his duties or to teach his disciples.

Much of his life remains a mystery, but we know he directed the course of the Theosophical Society from an esoteric school of adepts in a remote Himalayan valley inaccessible to anyone uninvited. Below him were advanced chelas (students). Above him were several chohans (lords, or masters) and the Maha Chohan. The strictest codes of esoteric discipline were kept.

Kuthumi taught with profound scholarship, and he had a mind able to penetrate the veils of time and read the *akashic* records of earth's history. The knowledge of his chohans was of intergalactic dimensions, and they guided him closely in all of his dealings with his chelas. Much to the wonder of his fellow adepts and to the consternation of his chohans, Kuthumi attempted to bring to Western man some of the long forbidden mysteries of the occult Brotherhood.

In a letter sent to the English Theosophist A. O. Hume in 1882, published in the book *The Mahatma Letters,*[1] Kuthumi wrote, "I would not refuse what I have a right to teach. Only I had to study for fifteen years before I came to the doctrines of cycles and had to learn simpler things at first."

Think of it! The master we have come to know and love as friend on the Path had to study fifteen years under the chohans before coming to the subject of the Law of Cycles. It is by dispensation of the Lords of Mind that we today shall penetrate some of these teachings, along with the revelations brought forth by the ascended masters.

Where shall we start our excursion through the vast ocean of God's creation? The wonder of it all is that no matter where we start, by following any cycle of life to its origin, there we stand gazing face-to-face with God. For he is the originator of all cycles. He is the driving force spinning at the pivot point of all form.

- 2 -

THE CYCLE DEFINED

A cycle is an interval of time during which a sequence of a recurring succession of events or phenomena is completed. It is also defined as a "recurrent sequence of events which occur in such order that the last event of one sequence immediately precedes the recurrence of the first event in a new series."

Place your hand on your heart and feel the cycles of your heart's pulsation, the beat of your physical life sustaining the vehicles of your soul's evolution in Matter.

Look up at a light bulb and know that it shines because electricity is pulsating at a cycle of sixty times per second through its filament.

Listen to a piece of music and hear the cyclic vibration of the violin strings resonating through the eardrum as sound.

All of cosmos can be comprehended in terms of cycles. The warp and woof of creation is manifest in currents of spiritual sound vibrating according to cyclic law. The very atoms and electrons of this world of form bow to the cyclic interchange of Spirit into Matter, Matter into Spirit—all-encompassed in the one element from which all of life issues forth.

The marriage of science and true religion brings forth the progeny of wisdom and higher understanding. Some of the elements of the Law of Cycles we will discuss clash with what is regarded as current scientific fact or archaeological proofs.

In the same letter of 1882 to Hume, in explaining how exact a science the esoteric teachings were, Kuthumi wrote, "Let me tell you that the means we avail ourselves of are all laid down for us in a code as old as humanity to the minutest detail, but every one of us has to begin from the beginning, not from the end. Our laws are as immutable as those of Nature, and they were known to man and eternity before this strutting gamecock, modern science, was hatched."

A hundred years have passed since that letter, and indeed the cycle has turned. Science is beginning to prove with her instruments and detectors many laws and facts previously considered to be occult meanderings.

CYCLES OF COSMOS

Cycles of man, nature, and cosmos often interact in the most remarkable and intricate ways. We see here graphic examples of the Hermetic axiom, As Above, so below, showing how the microcosmic cycles of man reflect the macrocosmic cycles of God, and how the processes of nature move with cyclic precision.

In Hindu philosophy there are four cyclic ages called *yugas* that follow one after another in the physical and spiritual evolution of man. It is said that the duration of our present *kali yuga* is 432,000 years. The combined duration of all four ages, each with a specific length, is 4,320,000. In one hour, our hearts beat 4,320 times, mirroring the 4-3-2 number that recurs in many other cycles as well.

The precession of the equinoxes is the time it takes the sun to make a complete circuit along the backdrop of the zodiacal constellations. This cycle takes 25,920 years to complete. In twenty-four hours, we breathe 25,920 times. The celestial cycle has its counterpart in the body of man.

Studies of the 11.1-year cycle of sunspots report that they are directly related to the magnetic conditions here on earth and correspond to peaks in the incidence of epidemics and social, economic, and political unrest.

Earthquakes also follow a cycle about eleven

years long. The greatest number of quakes occur about the same time as most sunspots. Also, irregularities in the earthquake cycle seem to correspond to irregularities in the sunspot cycle.

Japanese Dr. Maki Takata found that the composition of human blood changes in relation to the 11-year sunspot cycle, to solar flares, and during eclipses.

Changes in the earth's crust seem to correspond to the moon's position. It has been estimated that the city of Moscow rises and falls nearly twenty inches, twice a day, in response to the moon's gravitational pull.

Oysters rhythmically open their shells widest twice a day at high tide when the moon is exerting its maximum gravitational effect on the earth. One scientist removed oysters from New Haven, Connecticut to an Evanston, Illinois laboratory and noted that in about two weeks they had reset their motions to the Evanston lunar phases—opening their shells widest at the precise time when there would have been a high tide in Evanston if there had been an ocean. The oysters responded to the moon's force even though they were kept in a darkened room.

The grunion, a small fish of Southern California, spawn only when the tidal cycle is most favorable for the survival of its young. Every two weeks, from March to August, the grunion wiggle up onto the beach to lay and fertilize eggs on the night following the highest tide. In this way their eggs are undisturbed until the next high tide two weeks later when the egg membranes burst under the force of the waves to release the matured fish.

When researchers placed pieces of potato with sprouting eyes in a hermetically-sealed container in complete darkness and under constant pressure, they found that the potato had a 24-hour cycle of oxygen consumption directly related to the 24-hour cycle of barometric pressure outside the container. Most surprising was the potato's ability to accurately predict the outside barometric pressure two days in advance. With further experimentation, the researchers found that every living thing they studied —from carrots to seaweed, and from crabs and oysters to rats—could predict barometric pressure changes two days in advance.

Seemingly unrelated phenomena occur every 9.2 years. This interval marks cycles in grasshopper population, Lake Michigan water level, alternate thickness of tree rings, business failures, pig iron and copper prices, industrial stock prices, and railroad stock prices.

A
Ω

- 3 -

THE COSMIC MAGNET

To understand one of the basic tenets of the Law of Cycles, we must delve into the deepest mysteries of our Spirit-Matter universe. Here we contact the simplest and grandest of all cycles: the dual pulsation that is the heartbeat of cosmos. Here we find the one element, forever in equilibrium, forever pulsating in the rhythmic cycles that reverberate down to the inner core of every atom.

The entire religious philosophy of the yin/yang of Taoism is built upon the existence and importance of the cyclic interchange between an infinite hierarchy of opposing, or complementary, forces. It is the grand cycle of Alpha-to-Omega.

We hear it singing the song of the atom within our very own cosmos. It is the inhalation and exhalation of the Godhead. It is the interdimensional pattern of flow between Spirit and Matter—in Sanskrit, *Puruśa* and *Prakṛti*—the two poles of the cosmic magnet that sustains all of life. Truly, our study of the Law of Cycles is a meditation on our own inner Being.

We read in *The Path to the Higher Self,*[1] "The Truth all mankind seek is based on the irrefutable law that Spirit and Matter are not opposites: they are the twofold nature of God's Being which remain forever as the Divine Polarity."

This primary cycle we are considering is the simplest relationship of two forces—and the most all-encompassing action. If we clearly embrace the cyclic flow and unity between the Spirit-Matter, or Father-Mother principles of motion, it is as if we are given a library card to God's storehouse of universal knowledge.

As Kuthumi said, let us begin at the beginning, and all of the vast complexities of God's infinite cycles will become clear upon the illuminated background of the original cycle.

All form is the result of motion. To have motion implies a point toward which the motion occurs and away from which it proceeds. This, in its grandest conception, is the cosmic magnet, the Father-Mother flow.

A magnet attracts and a magnet repels. If you hold a horseshoe magnet in your hand, you can discover that there is a point of perfect equilibrium in the space exactly between the two opposite poles. At the heart of the polarity is unity and harmony.

All of cosmos is a magnet in the Macrocosmic sense. In his *Pearl of Wisdom* of June, 1968,[2] Sanat Kumara—known throughout religious literary history as "the Ancient of Days"—teaches about this cycle of universal flow:

> Those who would explore the far reaches of space, both inner and outer, should understand that the Divine Feminine is the womb of creation which is impregnated with life by the Spirit of God. The material universe is the negative polarity whereas the spiritual universe is the positive polarity of the Godhead. Matter, meaning *Mater* [Latin for Mother], is the chalice that receives the invigorating, life-giving essence of the sacred fire. Thus the Father principle

> completes the cycle of manifestation in the world of form through the Mother aspect, and child-man is nourished by the balancing, sustaining action of life whose twofold nature [Spirit/Matter, masculine/feminine] is epitomized in the Christ.

This divine polarity exists throughout cosmos—from the balanced pulsation of the Great Central Sun to the systemic equilibrium of the hydrogen atom.

We learn from the science of sound and from the archives of the Brotherhood that all manifested cosmos is the interplay of vibrations—a vast web of electromagnetic waves oscillating at different numbers of cycles per second. And what is a vibration if not a cyclic motion related to a framework of time and space orientation?

The range of cycles is infinite—from one cycle in billions of years to billions of cycles each second. All are derivatives of the one pulsation we observe pivoting around the point of infinite equilibrium of the cosmic magnet.

- 4 -

THE GRAND CYCLE

Before we become immersed in this web of creation, let us take a step up our mountain of observation and consider the grandest, longest, most mysterious cycle in the world of form. The length of this cycle is calculated in terms of trillions of years, and we find ourselves reaching for a volume that might be called the Life of Brahma.

Writing from the home of Kuthumi at Tzigadze in the Himalayas, gazing at an iceberg before him, Morya, one of the adepts who guided the Theosophical Society, wrote to A. P. Sinnett in January of 1882: "Nothing in nature springs into existence suddenly, all being subjected to the same law of gradual evolution. Realize but once the process of the maha cycle, of one sphere, and you have realized them all. One man is born like another man, one race evolves, develops, and declines like another and all other races. Nature follows the same groove from the 'creation' of a universe down to that of a mosquito. In studying esoteric cosmogony keep a spiritual eye upon the physiological process of human birth; proceed from cause to effect. . . . Cosmology is the physiology of the universe spiritualized, for there is but one law."

We will do just that. First we will learn of the cycles of Brahma, of God, as he unfolds the myriad systems of worlds. Then we will learn of man the microcosm. Eventually, the cycles of becoming will spread before us.

Man has always pondered the mysteries of creation. Scientists through the ages—astronomers, cosmologists, physicists—have developed various scenarios of the beginning of the universe.

The steady state theory postulates no beginning or ending—just a steady eternal state of non-transcendence.

The big bang theory states that around fifteen billion years ago all of matter we know of was compressed into an infinitely small ball of cosmic dust.

All of a sudden, the big bang—and the physical universe was born. The explosion occurred and life began to evolve from the atomic subparticle to our present universe.

Those who believe in this theory quietly hide their eyes from the question, "What came before the big bang? What was the cause behind the effect?"

Though the theory may explain one aspect of one cycle of cosmic evolution, it doesn't provide the framework for an integrated and all-embracing cosmo-conception.

Let us reach for the deeper perspective held in the retreats of the Brotherhood in the heart of the Himalayas. Not material scientists but great scientists of the Spirit, the ascended masters and cosmic beings can provide infant mankind with a perspective that spans endless eternities of creation.

In their view, the Law of Cycles is the key to the alternating cycles of the explosion and implosion of the Matter universes as they proceed in and out of Spirit.

THE MATHEMATICAL TRUTHS OF PYTHAGORAS

Pythagoras delivered the mathematical truths of the Law of Cycles to his spiritual community at Crotona, Italy in the sixth century B.C. All of cosmos, he taught, is comprehensible through numbers because the material universe is born from their very essence.

By knowing the numbers behind cosmic cycles, the initiate could approach a powerful understanding of the workings of the universe. So vast were the implications of this knowledge that the Pythagoreans kept it in strictest silence, sharing it with no uninitiated man.

This great master understood how music expressed the harmonic ratios of mathematics and used "musical medicine" to heal both body and soul.

Folio from a Bhagavata *Purāṇa* (Ancient Stories of the Lord)
Created: Late 18th century

- 5 -

EXPLORING THE *PURĀṆAS*

From the ancient epochs of India, history has preserved a series of writings called the *Purāṇas*. These are the teachings of great masters originally recorded in an extremely remote period in earth's history.

The word *Purāṇa* means "that which lives from ancient times," or "the records of ancient events." There are generally five subjects covered in these most ancient writings:

1. the creation of the universe;
2. re-creation after destruction or deluge;
3. the genealogy of the gods and teachers;
4. the *manvantaras*, or *Manu-antaras*, the great periods of time with the *Manu* as the primal ancestor; and, finally,
5. the histories of the Solar and Lunar dynasties.

One of the great Purāṇas is called the *Bhagavata Purāṇa*. In section III, the revered teacher Maitreya sets forth the revelation of the cycles of cosmic creation. He teaches about the days and nights of Brahma and the infinite cycles of beginnings and endings and new beginnings. We now shake the dust from this ancient text, totally neglected by Western historians, as we read these ancient records from Lord Maitreya to his pupil Vidura.

> O Vidura, beyond the three worlds . . . a day consists of one thousand cycles of four yugas. The night is also of the same duration when the creator of the universe goes to sleep. At the end of the night, the creation of the world starts and proceeds so long as it is God Brahma's day which covers the period of fourteen Manus.

In the chronology of the Hindus, one day of Brahma is said to be four billion, three hundred and twenty million years.

Continuing Maitreya's discourse to his pupil Vidura: "Every Manu rules during his own period which is somewhat longer than seventy-one cycles [each consisting] of four yugas."

A *yuga* is the Sanskrit word for a "world-period." The Sanskrit names for the four yugas are *Satya Yuga, Tretā Yuga, Dvāpara Yuga,* and *Kali Yuga.* Each successive age brings with it a different stage of civilization and a different mode of man's consciousness. In each of the yugas, man is given the spiritual tools that most effectively assist him to succeed in the cycles of evolution.

Just as the Great Cycle of Brahma's life is the archetype of man's personal cycles, so it is true with the yugas. The four yugas span millions of years in spheres of cosmic evolution, but we are taught that man himself goes through innumerable cycles of his own four yugas—as he walks the rounds toward reunion with God. We can compare the cycles of the evolution of the soul in the mastery of the four lower bodies, the four quadrants of being, with the cyclings of the four yugas. Thus the mastery of time and space is built upon this Law of Cycles.

One hundred cosmic years constitutes the life of Brahma. This is regarded as a whole period of Brahma's age, called the *Mahā Kalpa,* or "Great

Cycle." It is the longest single cycle we can detect. We are told that its duration is three hundred eleven trillion, forty billion years in length.

Maitreya continues in the *Bhagavata Purāṇa*, "Half of the life [of God Brahma] is called parārdha. The first parārdha [of his life] has passed. Now the other half is running." In our great cycle, our Mahā Kalpa, we have turned past the axial point of the course of cosmos.

God has once again exhaled his breath of life as *fohat* and the long inbreath has begun to return all to the spiritual source once again. The beginningless, endless cycle—as all things emanate from and return to the One.

God has neither beginning nor ending because his being takes in the universe of cycles and all that precedes and follows them in the formed and unformed dimensions of Spirit.

But for a brief interim man seems to have a beginning and an ending because he identifies with a slice of the spiral that initiates in Spirit, evolves through Matter, and returns to Spirit.

When outer man becomes congruent with the

Figure 1

spiritual essence of his own Divine Monad, he then becomes the drop merging into the ocean of God. Our individualized personalities had a beginning in the warp and woof of manifestation, but the core of the atom of our being, our spiritual Monad, began when God himself began.

THE CHAIN OF CYCLES

In figure 1, you see a chain of cycles placed on a grid of the golden ratio. Imagine that you are floating above this expanding spiral, looking down into its receding central cycle—which disappears into the infinite past. Each cycle of evolution takes in more of God. Each round sends you into wider spheres of the body of God's cosmos.

Each new emergence from the period of *pralaya* brings you into a new, higher creation, ever spiraling upwards from glory unto glory—into the endless realms of infinity.

With perfect mathematical precision these cycles follow the vast spiral of transcendence based upon the golden ratio. (See chapter 12 *The Golden Ratio*)

- 6 -

THE LAW OF KARMA

The Law of Karma, of perfect retribution, is intimately related to the Law of Cycles.

We can know with absolute surety that if we send out hatred or negative vibrations, sooner or later they will cycle back to ourselves and we will have to expend energy to revibrate our murky creation.

We can also know that the self-generated impulse toward God, toward good, toward service of our fellowman will, with infinite precision, cycle back also and add to our momentum of light and our return to wholeness. This is the Law of Karma. It is the mathematically predictable Law of Cycles. It is the most simple yet profound manifestation of justice.

By willingly coming into congruence with the cycle of involution, evolution, and ascension, we know that at the end of this round we will indeed see the face of God.

Can we imagine what it would be like if the Law of Cycles didn't exist, if we had no way of knowing where to direct our striving to return to a state of wholeness?

To recapitulate what we have learned, there is the endless rhythmic pulsation of cosmic creation called in the East the Mahā Kalpa, or Great Cycle. Though there are infinite cycles within cycles, the overall flow consists of an outbreath and an inbreath, an Alpha thrust of creation followed by the Omega return to the heart of Brahma. At the end of each creative cycle is the *pralaya,* which is the Sanskrit word for the "period of rest." At best, then, the big bang theory becomes a crude statement of the sublime cosmic moment of the birth of worlds when the sine wave passes from imperceptible to perceptible reality—that is, from what we call Spirit to what we call Matter.

Delving deeper into the mysteries of creation, we come to the awareness that all is Spirit. All forms of Matter—even the densest physical substance—are the crystallized fire mist of spiritual essence. The successive lives of Brahma can be conceived of by our limited minds as immense cyclic arcs of pure Spirit involuting into the veils of denser Matter, and then evoluting back to the ethereal, spiritual origin.

Our relative position in the grand cycle of our personal or planetary cycle can be understood as the ratio of Spirit to Matter. As Brahma outbreathes the web of creation, there is a densification as the universe puts on its seven coats of skins.

An axial point is reached in the cycle where the outbreath is expended and inbreath begins. It is the point of the lowest descent of the arc of Spirit into Matter. It is the state of equilibrium of the positive and negative poles of the cosmic magnet. It is the halfway point in the cycle that Maitreya mentioned we have passed.

Then there is the period of return to Spirit. All that has become involved in material form begins its process of etherealization and return to the one

Source—and to the period of pralayic rest—once again to begin a new cycle of becoming.

THE SECRET OF THE LAW OF CYCLES

The simple diagram (Figure 2) helps us to understand the great secret of the Law of Cycles. The point in the center of the circle (Point C) is the *laya center*, the etheric neutral point. We can describe this center as the nirvanic disassociation of all form merging all into primordial *akasha*.

The cycle flows from top to bottom in a regular sine wave forming the pattern known as the T'ai Chi. The central point of the cycle is the point of transition between the Alpha thrust and the Omega return.

It is said in *The Secret Doctrine*[1] that "whatsoever quits the laya state becomes active life; it is drawn into the vortex of motion; Spirit and Matter are the two equilibrized states." All atoms issue forth from the center point of the creative pulsation of the Godhead, and every one of those atoms has its own neutral center. As Above, so below.

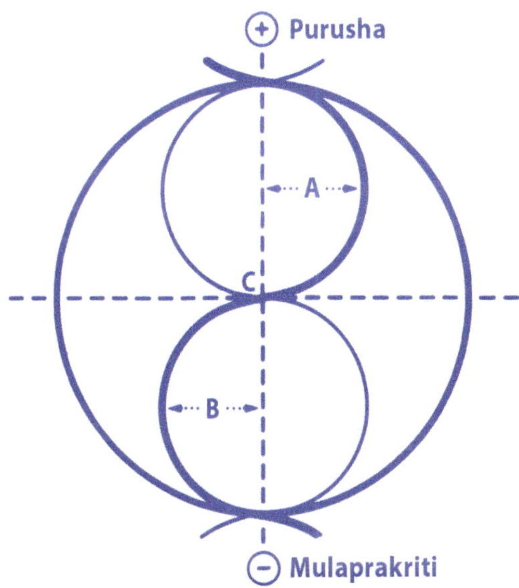

Figure 2

This diagram (Figure 3) symbolizes cycles within cycles ad infinitum. The vertical line in the middle (called A–B) represents the neutral center common to all cycles in cosmos. It is the axial point in the secret chamber of God's creative heart.

All cycles, all vibrations, and therefore all Matter varies according to the frequency and angle of deviation from the neutral, balanced, undifferentiated laya center.

The most common form of electricity is a cyclic flow of a form of akasha vibrating 60 times each second. The magnitude of potential energy, called voltage, is a function of how far away from the neutral center of the cycle the energy has been made to flow. The greater the distance, the more energy available because there is a greater polarity built between the plus and minus crests of the cycle. The same is true in the world of man and Spirit. Man can send out greater or lesser vibrations of energy from the power center in his heart.

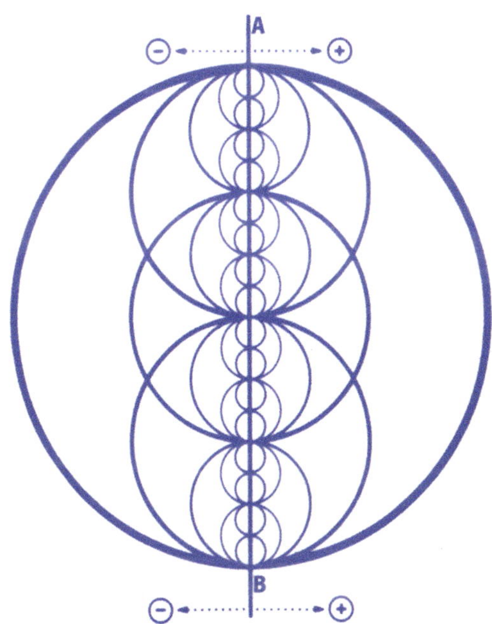

Figure 3

- 7 -

THE LAWS OF TRANSCENDENCE AND CORRESPONDENCE

The process of self-transcendence, or the spiritual evolution of consciousness, was typified by Leonardo da Vinci's famous illustration of archetypal man experiencing the squaring of the circle. Here the cube represents Matter and finite three-dimensional consciousness; the sphere represents Spirit and the infinite, multidimensional consciousness.

Through the golden-ratio formation of spheres, we can contemplate evolution proceeding from an infinite past to an infinite future, with man moving in the cycles of cosmos as he himself becomes a sphere in the self-transcending body of God. We might say that Man in his highest expression of Self is the culmination of the golden ratio of cosmic consciousness.

THE LAW OF TRANSCENDENCE

As we ponder the immense odyssey of God's being through eternal rounds of beginnings and endings, we can ask the fateful question: Why? What is the purpose of it all if the universe is just an endless cycle of rounds with man floating on a speck of dust in space cast loose on a shoreless ocean? What is the nature of the Godhead as he exists through endless cycles in infinite space?

The answer, we are told, is that the Law of Cycles implements the Law of Transcendence. God is a transcendent being, and with each new out-breath he evolves to a greater state of cosmic perfection and beauty.

The cycles are not really circles or sine waves but they are spirals—spirals of infinite expansion according to the geometry of the golden ratio (1:1.618...). Each cycle of evolution takes in more of God. Each round sends us into wider spheres of the body of God's cosmos.

The individualities enmeshed in the fabric of the Godhead eventually reach a point in evolution where they span the cyclic lifetimes of Brahma. With each new pulsation, after each successive pralaya, the imprint of higher planes of perfection impregnate the gestating cosmic egg.

The endless cyclic patterns of cosmic evolution would be an abominable injustice if not for the fact that each new cycle begins at a higher point of perfection. This universe is not an infernal merry-go-round that spins in space.

What meaningless boredom, what hellish drudgery it would be to have to return forever to the same place in the cycle like a broken record. God and all of his creation is continually transcending itself, with the leading edge of consciousness always able to contact new vistas of infinity and to create greater manifestations of divine purpose.

How does man the individual fit into this vast cosmic plan of transcendent cycles? How can we apply the Law of Cycles for the purpose of greater acceleration around the rings of initiation?

THE LAW OF CORRESPONDENCE

In the far-distant past, Hermes, Messenger of the Gods, delivered to us the nucleus of the Law of Cycles—"As Above, so below."

We still retain what is called the "Emerald Tablet" of Hermes. This short but concise teaching formed the core of the most ancient masonic orders and schools of the Brotherhood. It begins with these words:

> True, without any error;
> certain, very true;
> That which is Above,
> is as that which is below;
> and that which is below,
> is as That which is Above;
> For achieving the wonders
> of the Universe.

This is the Law of Analogy, the Law of Correspondence, and it provides us with the sense of divine order, which is indeed the sense of justice.

The Law of Correspondence states that the creation corresponds to the Creator, that man corresponds to God. Therefore, the Real Image of man is congruent with his God Source by design, by intent, by Law.

The design is one of transcendent cycles, mirrored all the way through the veils of Matter into the coil of the densest atom.

The intent is for man the individual to become a beneficent co-creator with the Godhead, to span cosmic cycles, to be the one who breathes out galactic systems and provides the impulse of coherent love that binds the particulate atoms into a meaningful platform of evolution.

The Law is the law of recurrent cycles ever transcending the previous round. The Law of Transcendence offers us the comfort of the highest hope.

As the cycles of cosmos spiral upward into greater and greater dimensions, so man can forever transcend the veils of Matter that form the schoolrooms for his soul's evolution. The transcendent teaching of the Christ reveals infinite possibilities for God and man. It destroys the lie of eternal damnation. It opens the door of opportunity for repentance and healing. It is absolute justice in manifestation.

It is not easy for mortal man to stretch his mind beyond the boundaries of infinity. Maitreya has taught that a lifetime of Brahma, a universe lasting trillions of years, appears as a single atom when merged in the body of the great Puruśa. The planets spinning around our sun are like one atom in the body of the Milky Way galaxy—the galaxy having over a hundred billion sun centers, each with its own system of worlds. The being ensouling the galaxy is aware of our world as an atom in his body, teeming with sentient life evolving.

And then there is man—the oversoul and God to a vast universe of his inner identity. We are cells in the body of God, and we have fifty trillion cells that compose our body. Each one of those cells has intelligence, has a spark of divinity. Think of it. Each one of our cells considers us as the Godhead of its universe, the originator of its life impulses. Paul said, "Know ye not that ye are the temple of God, and that the Spirit of God dwelleth in you?"

How far along the vibratory spectrum of cosmic life can we go in each direction?

Who is to say that there isn't a complex system of life-forms resident on the surface of each electron as it spins in polar equilibrium to its nuclear sun center—just as our earthy sphere of cosmic dust spins around its sun, teeming with life? The mortal mind cannot tell. But beings with vast awareness have told us that the cycles of God are infinite in all directions.

Let us consider man the microcosm, who is also the Macrocosm, and behold the workings of cyclic law as we trace the course of man's evolution in the hierarchical ladder of being.

Let us first consider man and his indivisible parts and define thereby which portion of man travels along the endless cycles of evolution.

- 8 -

MAN—THE MICROCOSM

Man is a sevenfold creation. The Great White Brotherhood has always taught that the number seven is the primary harmonic quantity. Man is composed of seven sheaths, or bodies, bestowed upon him by the Lords of Form who, in turn, are sevenfold in their own nature.

Pythagoras explained the theory of the eternal Monad to his inner disciples. According to the adept Kuthumi, the reincarnation of Master Pythagoras, the Monad can be considered as the upper two principles of man's sevenfold being.

It is this reflective spark of divinity that sends forth our soul to cycle through the veils of maya. And through the threefold flame this soul constructs around itself the temporary lower vehicles used to draw in experience of God's nature. It is the sacred fire infolding more and more of itself.

The Divine Monad exists even after the transition called death, while the lower bodies dissipate according to the cyclic laws of their substance. All of substance in Matter is subject to the Law of Cycles governing integration and disintegration, or the manifestation of form and the return to formlessness.

The soul is the as-yet-nonpermanent atom in God's body. It is infused with the germinal seed to become ruler of a cosmos. This it must do by the exercise of free will.

It is the soul as the extension of the I AM Presence and causal body that is given opportunity to spin the "Deathless Solar Body" out of the fibers of akasha.

THE CIRCLE OF LIFE

The riddle of eternity and evolution is contained within the symbol of the circle—a cross section of a spiral that has neither beginning nor ending but appears to be finite as it passes through the physical universe in the form of planets, stars, galaxies, and man himself.

The circle is the two-dimensional representation of the spiral cycle that begins in the square base of the pyramid and rises to the apex of realization in the capstone of life. And there in the center of the capstone, the Law of Transcendence functions through the eye of God. For when the spiral passes through the all-seeing eye, it transcends the dimensions of form and passes from Matter to Spirit.

This is the fulfillment of the Law of Cycles that begins in the heart of God and culminates in every perfect creation. Energy that begins as a spiral in Spirit descends into Matter, there to coalesce around the flame and then—in the twinkling of an eye—to return to Spirit over the descending and ascending spirals of God's consciousness. God himself is the circle that has neither beginning nor ending of cycles, though we can detect the pulsations of his inbreath and outbreath.

The heavenly bodies are undergoing cyclic evolution within the larger infinite spiral of God's being in Spirit—passing through material manifestation and returning to Spirit. In the Macrocosm as well as in the microcosm, circling spirals trigger the flow of energy into and out of form.

Throughout the universe, the pattern of cyclic return is reproduced again and again with infinite precision, traversing realms of eternity, expanding according to the golden ratio.

- 9 -

MAN AS CO-CREATOR

Although the circle itself is without beginning or ending, at any point on the circumference of the circle, the hand of God may draw an intersecting line, thereby creating a beginning and an ending. Thus cycles are initiated and worlds are born.

The whirl of fohatic release, directed by the guiding will of a God-free being, can send reverberating vibrations careening through space. Drop a stone into a still pond and watch the cyclic wave patterns continue to flow and flow in smooth rhythm. Drop a stone into an agitated pond, and there results a complex of wave pattern interchange, but the cycle initiated by the stone continues to affect the water. Thus it is by the hand of God and by his emissaries.

Once man has passed through the cycles of the initiatic process—the spirals of destiny that unlock the total pattern of his identity—he earns the right to be congruent with the dot in the center of the great circle of life. That dot in the center of the circle is the point of dynamic equilibrium resident in all of creation.

There is always that central point of balance, called the laya center in Hindu esoteric science. To become one with this power center, this dot of equilibrium in the center of God's circle, is to be able to direct the power of fohat as it courses along the vibratory pathways we create.

Visualize a simple sine wave (Figure 4). This represents a rhythmic cycle of a particular frequency. There is a rising curve, then a falling curve, and then a rising curve, and so forth. According to the Law of Cycles, there must be a force that pulls the current of God's undifferentiated energy into the rising curve. And there must be an opposite force that attracts this stream of energy (represented by the line) into the falling curve. These are the positive and negative poles active at the core of all cycles.

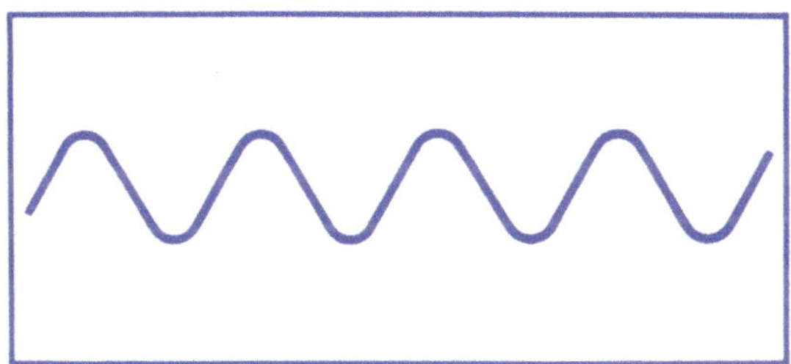

Figure 4

To be the dot in the center of the circle is to become the harmony of the polar forces—to be the axis in the spinning sphere of creative force. It is the pivot point of cyclic flow. It is reached in samadhi. It is utilized by adepts to control the fire of space.

All of manifested cosmos is the interplay of cyclic vibrations, initiated somewhere, somehow, by someone. As we ascend the scales of evolution, we are entrusted with the divine power and authority to initiate cycles that may last forever.

If you find the point of balance anywhere in cosmos, you can travel unperturbed through the successive neutral centers all the way to the center of the Great Central Sun. All the centers of all the cycles are congruent in the highest dimension of cosmos. Find one center and you have found them all. Find your first love and you have found all loves. Remain at the point of balance, of perfect love, and you reside in the heart of God.

This great secret pathway through the tunnels of cyclic equilibrium, designed into the fabric of life, is God's great gift to man. Become the dot in the center of his circle, correspond to the pulsation of his heart, and look forward to infinite horizons of beauty and perfectionment.

- 10 -

THE MOLDING OF SUBSTANCE

The ancient wisdom teaches us that there is one element, one cosmic substance—akasha—from which all form is made. It is fluidic in motion, ethereal, and interpenetrates all substance. Without weight, without color of its own, it takes on the properties of vibratory patterns imposed upon it—patterns that can be impressed on it by sound and by thought.

Even Spirit has form. As we recede into the eternal depths of creation and rise into infinitely higher planes of consciousness, still there is form—and all conforms to the Law of Cycles.

All substance, all form, all life is the result of force causing Matter to move. *Force Causes Matter to Move.* Force can be generated voluntarily, consciously, by an intelligent being. The infinite hierarchy of ascended beings turns the wheels and cycles of worlds by the force of their will. Brahma uses force to mold galaxies. The masters use force to mold ideas and create the various pockets of life in the universe.

Force can also be the impulse of the unconscious, meticulously accurate mechanism that drives the substratum of the material planes. Matter cannot be divorced from Spirit.

In order to have motion, there must be a medium through which vibrations can occur. The fluid nature of akasha responds to vibrational force in a wavelike, cyclic flow—just like the pebble thrown into the fluid pond. Motion is the alteration of akasha that is inherently in a state of harmony, of rest, of equilibrium. Apply any force into the ocean of akasha and cycles of motion result.

The myriad forms we see in the universe are the conglomerate wave patterns resulting from simple or complex combinations of sine waves moving in cycles. The days and nights of Brahma, if symbolized in two dimensions, would be an even, rhythmic flow between the two poles of the cosmic magnet. The allness of the one element is driven into motion by the will of God.

Scientists Douglas Vogt and Gary Sultan have approached the inner workings of this Law of Cycles. They postulate in their book *Reality Revealed* that all of the physical elements are brought into our plane by the interaction of cyclic waveforms. The simplest form of motion is represented by the sine wave. The diagram below (Figure 5) represents sine waves interacting in two planes of angular dimension.

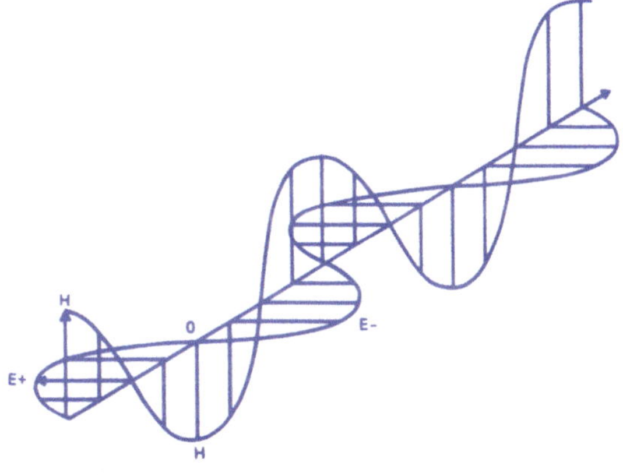

Figure 5

SCIENCE AND THE LAYA CENTER

The conception of the ascended masters is, of course, complete, whereas few scientists have penetrated the mystery of the point of balance, the laya center. Nikola Tesla found the power at the neutral center of all cycles—and proceeded to conceptualize devices that would perpetually run on the cyclic vibrations of our planetary sphere as it pulsates with a heartbeat of its own. Unfortunately for us, Tesla's motor was never developed for public use.

Tesla was not the only one who discovered the power at the center of the circle. One of the greatest scientists of all time, ironically unknown to our modern clan of quark-seekers, was Mr. John Worrell Keely of Philadelphia.

Quoted in *The Secret Doctrine* of H. P. Blavatsky, in explanation of an engine he designed, Mr. Keely says:

> In the conception of any machine heretofore constructed, the medium for inducing a neutral center has never been found. If it had, the difficulties of perpetual-motion seekers would have

ended, and this problem would have become an established and operating fact. It would only require an introductory impulse of a few pounds, on such a device, to cause it to run for centuries. In the conception of my vibratory engine, I did not seek to attain perpetual motion; but a circuit is formed that actually has a *neutral center,* which is in a condition to be vivified by my vibratory ether, and, while under operation by said substance, is really a machine that is virtually independent of the mass (or globe), and it is the wonderful velocity of the vibratory circuit that makes it so.

Still, with all its perfection, it requires to be fed with the vibratory ether to make it an independent motor. . . . All structures require a foundation in strength according to the weight of the mass they have to carry, but the foundations of the universe rest on a vacuous point far more minute than a molecule; in fact, to express this truth properly, on an *inter-etheric point,* which requires an infinite mind to understand it.

To look down into the depths of an etheric

> center is precisely the same as it would be to search into the broad space of heaven's ether to find the end, with this difference: that one is the positive field, while the other is the negative field.

Here we have the marriage of the science of Matter with the laws of Spirit. This etheric neutral point, balanced between the positive and negative, is the dot suspended in the center of the circle of God's being.

- 11 -

THE POINT OF PEACE

As man evolves through the folds of time and space, the key to safe passage through the initiatic tests is harmony and balance. The vicissitudes of life can all be viewed objectively from the balance point in the center of our heart, which is congruent with the center of God's heart. We can move through all cycles and not be removed from this stable point if we but apply this science of cycles.

To illustrate this, visualize an ordinary seesaw in a playground. It is a flat board resting on a central pivot point. As a child mounts on each end of the board, they create a cyclic movement that would look like a sine wave if represented in a graph. But notice that the center of the board, the center of the cycle, is absolutely stationary. The children can be moving wildly, frantically on the ends, and the center is always balanced and stable.

Thus it is with all cycles, and thus it can be through all of life. This cyclic center in man is the heart chakra, as we see in Figure 6.

The body of man is a magnet. This has been proven by scientists and spiritual healers alike. We recall that all magnets create cycles of positive and negative flow, yet there is always a point of perfect equilibrium between the two polarities. The heart is that point of equilibrium as prana flows through our system. There is a place of perfect harmony in the secret chamber of the heart, which is beyond the physical heart, pulsating in cyclic rhythm seventy-two times a minute every day of our lives.

This is why the masters tell us to go there, to go to this point of balance in our hearts. Because there is the point of peace. But it is also the point of power.

Figure 6

RETURN THROUGH THE WORD

The path of the ascension is the means whereby sons of God preserve an identity as a single cell in the being of Brahma throughout the pralayas and throughout the inhalation and the exhalation of God.

As we noted earlier, in each yuga, man is given specific spiritual tools to assist him in his evolution.

It is said that we are presently in a Kali Yuga—a cycle of returning karma, the darkest of all four of the cycles. Sanat Kumara, the Great Guru, assigns forms of communion with God that are befitting the evolutions of man with the yugas.

Sanat Kumara has told us that in this yuga, the key to contact God is the science of the spoken Word. Using this science, practiced by adepts East and West for thousands of years, we can send forth auric emanations from the point of power within the center of our heart to heal our personal microcosm and the world outside the boundary of our skin.

To endure as a cell in the consciousness of God when that God is at perfect rest is to enter with him into the cosmic cycle of nirvana. To do this, one must pass through the nexus of the cycle—the Word.

The eternal Logos is the dot in the center of the circle, the beginning and ending of cycles that are composed of circles, layer upon layer.

In the beginning was Brahma, and the Word was with Brahma, and the Word was with Brahma in the beginning. Therefore, in order to be in Brahma, we must be in the Word. "No man cometh to the Father but by me." That "me" is the supreme I AM THAT I AM manifest as the Word.

It is a swaddling garment wound around about the earth. The very currents of the earth's surface, the very emanations from its sun center, the Law of Cycles, the comfort flame, the hum just below the level of our own hearing transfers to us this comfort of the cyclic law of the sounding of God's Word.

Life is ongoing, and the Law of Cycles promises us that life will go on. God's heart will beat on. The wheel of cyclic return will rotate on the spokes of our karmic creations.

By the Law of Cycles, then, we are set upon our courses spiraling through once again the nexus of being, the nexus being the Word itself, the Law of Cycles being the emanation of the Word. As we become congruent with the dot in the center of God's circle, the power is bestowed upon us to imprint the cyclic energies of God with the pattern of our God-oriented idea or desire.

This is the way to return to God as a permanent atom in his being—through this Word that has incarnated in the avatars with the cyclic law of manifestation. The great Manus, the lawgivers of the ages and of their races, upheld the cycle of the Word whereby all seed going forth from the great Tree of Life might return through the Word as the Law of Cycles.

There is joy in this Law of Cycles. And the joy of this marriage of science and religion is you at the nexus of infinity, you converging with that living Word.

- 12 -

THE GOLDEN RATIO

FORMULAS FOR TRANSCENDENCE

Indelibly inscribed in the heart of nature and man is a mathematical formula for growth and transcendence: the golden ratio.

Trace the thread of this "golden mean" from daisy to pyramid, from pinecone to Parthenon. . . . Or follow it from a tiny spiraled seashell to spiral nebulae forty million times the size of the sun. The cosmos weaves its garments with perfect integrity, laced by the golden ratio.

This ratio is a specific mathematical proportion that is so omnipresent that many philosophers, artists, mathematicians, and scientists have considered it an essential component of beauty, perhaps integral to life itself. Plato considered it the key to the physics of cosmos. The Egyptians thought it more than a number and believed it symbolized the creative process and the fire of life.

This magical golden proportion is found by dividing a line (AC) at a particular point to yield two unequal sections, where the smaller one (AB) is proportionate to the larger one (BC) as the larger one (BC) is to the entire line (AC). The ratio is expressed as:

There is only one such point (B) on any line. The ratio between the two sections is always the same on any length line: 1:1.618..., known as ϕ or "phi."

The amount of numbers after the decimal point is endless. Phi is what is called an irrational number because man can only approximate the exact figure. A computer making one million calculations each second for a billion years would never reach the precise golden ratio. This is because phi represents a divine ideation—an etheric formula for transcendence and beauty superimposed by the

Creator upon the physical plane. The essence of this ratio operates in a higher dimension, and so finite numbers cannot perfectly contain this infinite principle.

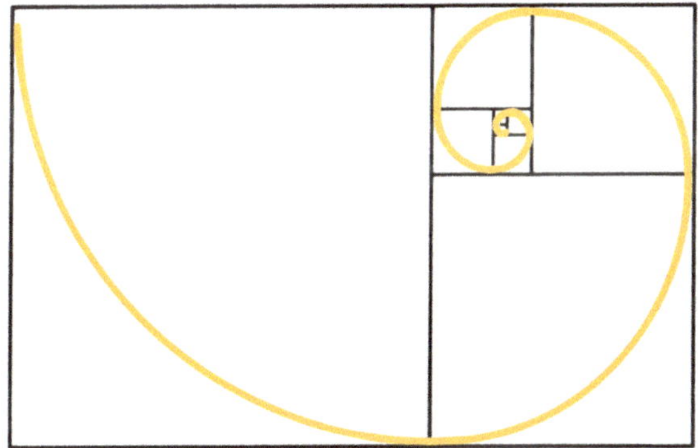

The phi ratio incorporated in a "golden rectangle" yields an infinite progression of smaller and smaller golden rectangles, each with the same potential for phi subdivision.

The phi points of each rectangle can be connected to form a logarithmic "golden spiral" dubbed by mathematicians *spira mirabilis*—"the wondrous spiral."

The spiral's open end seems to thrust majestically forward and outward, ever widening in its dynamic expression of life. According to English author Theodore Andrea Cook, the golden spiral is the original inspiration for the oriental T'ai Chi, a symbol of life once used by twelfth-century Chinese philosophers. The two curved halves of the T'ai Chi, says Cook, are portions of the logarithmic (phi proportion) curve copied by man from the abundantly available nautilus shell.

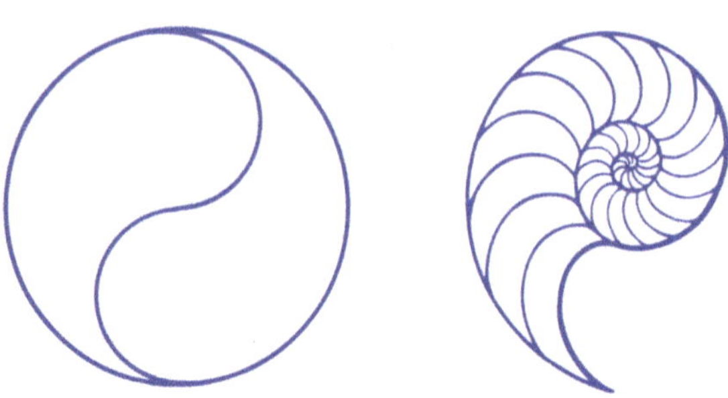

Man has displayed a perennial fascination—both conscious and subconscious—with the golden ratio. Egyptian pyramids and Gothic cathedrals use the mathematical functions of phi in the heights, widths, and angles of their outer walls and internal chambers. Greece's classical architects designed the Parthenon to fit a golden rectangle. Virgil, it appears, wrote his epic *Aeneid* in the phi ratio, arranging his poetic passages with mathematical precision.

Renaissance artists also made abundant use of this ratio. Da Vinci's famous conception of man within the squaring of the circle describes man's body in terms of phi—a fact of human anatomy known since Egyptian times. Phi proportions fill the works of Raphael, Titian, Luini, and Veronese, defining both the architectural designs and the living figures in their compositions.

But it is more than coincidence that phi endures as a symbol of life and beauty in art and architecture. The golden ratio describes with numbers and geometry the universal formula for growth. Its resulting pentagonal symmetry (using phi angles) is not naturally found in inorganic, "inanimate" forms like crystals or snowflakes but only in living forms.

Inanimate systems are governed by the "principle of least action" though they, too, have a special beauty. But living, organic systems seem to opt for a "principle of greatest action," expanding in golden-spiral growth patterns or in geometries of phi ratios—constantly transcending the static, least-action principles of the inanimate.

But why does life express itself in certain consistent mathematical patterns—especially the golden ratio?

Pythagoras must have asked a similar question 2,500 years ago. In an effort to encapsulate his spiritual explorations of the vast mysteries of the cosmos, he declared simply, "All is number." For Pythagoras, number was intimately connected with man's psyche. Man's soul is a kind of harmony, as Pythagoras noted, and is affected by the "vibrations"—the numbers—of the surrounding world.

This principle is basic. Distort the vibrations of the world—by distorting art, architecture, and music—and the tenor of man's soul will reflect the disharmony. But construct the world through perfection in the arts, using the concordant vibrations of pleasing numerical ratios, and man's soul will reflect the harmony evoked by his surroundings.

The golden ratio, as nature demonstrates, is the

foundation of organic harmony. The cosmos is naturally governed by the harmonious phi—indeed, the Greek word *kosmos* once implied an ordered harmony.

In certain periods of earth's history, man learned to use the harmonious principles of phi to a great degree. With a knowledge now mostly lost to man, master architects once used the power of the golden ratio in constructing pyramids and temples not as tombs, but as focuses of spiritual energy used for purposes yet beyond our understanding.

The sacred science of its use may be temporarily diminished, but the golden ratio peers out at us from every corner of the world. Its repeated manifestations seem a constant reminder of those secrets it contains for us, always inviting our further investigation.

The mollusk known as the chambered nautilus houses itself in a golden-spiral shell. Still smaller, water molecules hold oxygen and hydrogen atoms at a specific angle (104°) derived from phi. This ratio formulates the components of the matter cosmos from the periodicity of atomic elements to colossal spiral nebulae.

Though these vast and microscopic dimensions are invisible to the naked eye, we need only look in our backyards to find the same evidence. Back in the thirteenth century, Leonardo Fibonacci did so—and this distinguished mathematician of the Middle Ages uncovered the numerical sequence generated by the golden ratio.

Pentagonal symmetry is common in flowers, demonstrating several combinations of golden-ratio properties. The lines of the pentagram, emblem of the ancient Pythagorean brotherhood, intersect each other at phi points.

This sequence of numbers (1,1,2,3,5,8,13,21. . .) is interesting in itself because each term of the series is the sum of the two preceding terms. The ratio of each term to its previous term gets closer to the golden ratio as the numbers get larger, as shown in this table.

Term	Prior Term	Ratio
1	1	1
2	1	2
3	2	1.5
5	3	1.66...
8	5	1.6
13	8	1.625
21	13	1.615...
34	21	1.619...
55	34	1.617...
89	55	1.618...

The application of the Fibonacci sequence is vast, since it defines innumerable natural processes from the genealogy of male honeybees to the scales of a pineapple.

Phyllotaxy (the arrangement of leaves on a stem) follows the precise Fibonacci sequence. Branches of the sneezewort subdivide according to Fibonacci rules. Flowers blossom into pentagonal shapes, exhibiting phi angles. Sunflower heads and daisies crown the family of phi patterns with their display of two interwoven golden-ratio spirals.

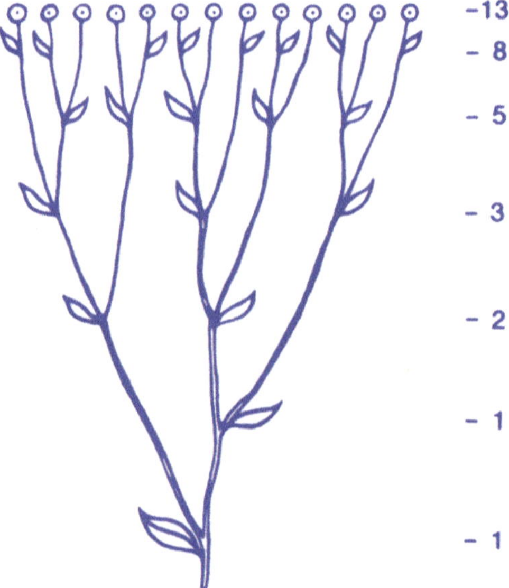

Sneezewort (Achillea ptarmica)

The visible universe grows in a body of golden proportions.

The prominent ratio is also audible. Music, the acoustic progeny of mathematics, partakes of the "golden mean." Most listeners prefer the musical interval of the "major sixth"—whose frequency ratio (between the low and high notes) approximates phi proportion.

From botany to music, from matter to sound—where does this continuum of vibrations, of numbers, lead? By logical extension it gestures upward to higher frequencies perceptible only to the soul. And if the golden ratio governs growth in the physical universe, might it not also govern man's spiritual growth?

When we devise a way to chart our psychological and spiritual growth patterns, we might well find that they also expand along the logarithmic golden spiral. How many times have we found ourselves in a repeated situation—but, older and a little wiser, on a higher arm of the spiral of our growth, looking back "down" at our previously limited understanding of that situation?

The spiral of the learning process beckons us ever onward to higher-level "classrooms" where the lessons are refined.

In the dynamic momentum of this formula for transcendence, that which stands still or refuses to progress in its "lessons" inevitably stagnates and loses step with the cosmic cycles of life. In order to survive, one must unceasingly pursue the upward swing of his inner potential.

If this observation of our growth is true, then perhaps He, too, thus grows—the Creator whose insignia we bear. With each new outbreath in the endless succession of manvantaric cycles of cosmos, all of creation transcends its former state in accordance with the golden ratio.

The mathematics of beauty. The keynote of the music of the spheres. The formula for soul transcendence. Follow the spiraling golden thread upward with your eyes, your ears, and your heart, and see how far you can go.

- 13 -

MATHEMATICS OF BEAUTY

The School of Athens, masterpiece of Raphael, is a perfect example of the use of the golden ratio in Renaissance painting. Plato and Aristotle (center) and the many famous philosophers represent the Athenian school of thought, which long ago understood and used the golden mean. The painting is centralized and symmetrical in precise golden-ratio geometry. Several golden rectangles are embodied in the composition, and dozens of its angles (created by the figures and the architecture) are made according to the phi ratio.

Renaissance artist Raphael composed his famous *Madonna of the Chair* in the golden phi proportions. The overlay of the lines of emphasis show the formation of two intersecting pentagrams.

The human face reflects the golden-ratio geometry, as shown in this bust of Aphrodite.

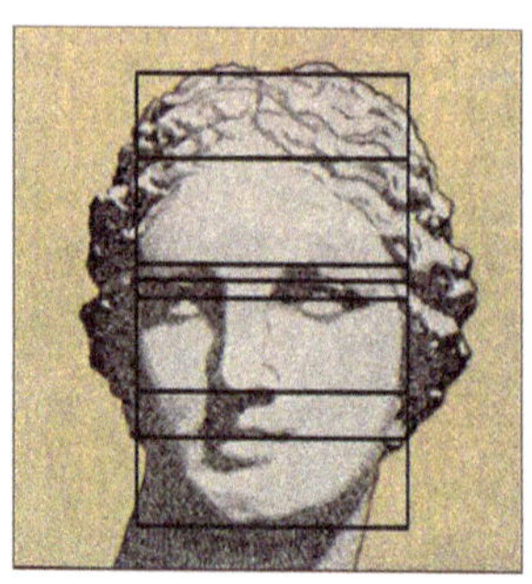

Violin heads have long followed the curve of the golden spiral.

Music can express the golden ratio in the major sixth, a fundamental musical interval.

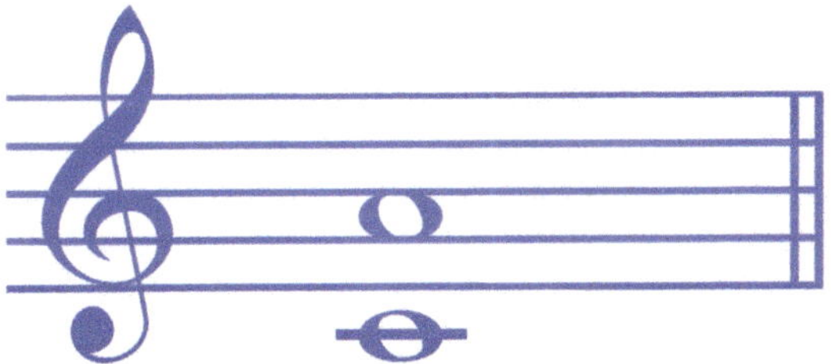

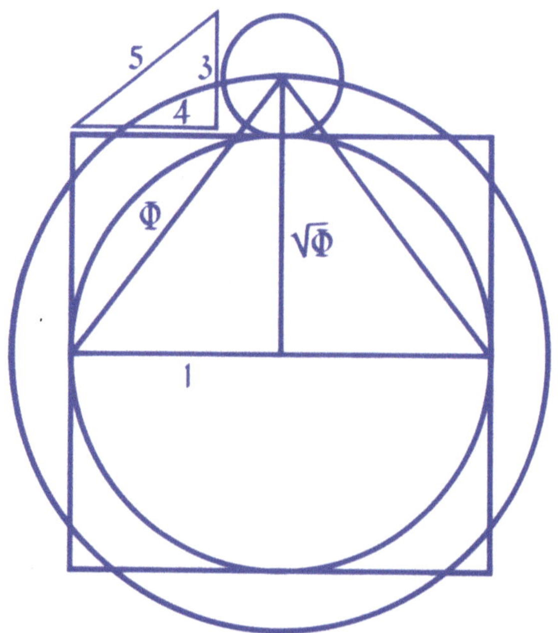

The line diagram above shows the workings of phi in the geometry of the Great Pyramid, which also embodies the mathematical relationship of the earth and moon.

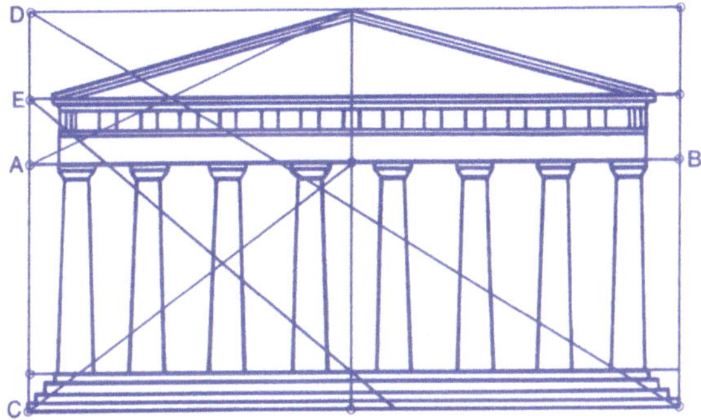

The Parthenon in Athens, the epitome of classical Greek architecture, embodies golden-ratio principles. Its frontal design is a golden rectangle; the ratio of the distance from the top of the columns to the bottom step (AC) and the top of the columns to the top of the pediment (AD) is a golden ratio. Likewise, the height of the pediment itself (ED) is in the golden proportion (phi) to the height of the lintel and friezes (AE).

NOTES

CHAPTER 1

1. The masters M. and K.H. wrote *The Mahatma Letters* between 1880 and 1884 to A. P. Sinnett, a disciple in the Theosophical Society.

CHAPTER 3

1. *The Path to the Higher Self* by Mark L. Prophet and Elizabeth Clare Prophet, Summit University Press.
2. *Pearls of Wisdom,* "The Space Within," June 23, 1968.

CHAPTER 6

1. *The Secret Doctrine: The Synthesis of Science, Religion, and Philosophy,* two volumes by H. P. Blavatsky, Theosophical University Press.

224 pp • ISBN 978-0-922729-61-6

Karma and Reincarnation

Transcending Your Past, Transforming Your Future

The word *karma* has made it into the mainstream. But not everyone knows what it really means or how to deal with it. This insightful book will help you come to grips with karmic connections from past lives that have helped create the circumstances of your life today. You'll discover how your actions in past lives—good and bad—affect which family you're born into, who you're attracted to, and why some people put you on edge. You'll learn about group karma, what we do between lives, and what the great lights of East and West, including Jesus, have to say about karma and reincarnation. Most of all, you'll find out how to turn your karmic encounters into grand opportunities to shape the future you want.

160 pp • ISBN 978-0-922729-55-5

The Art of Practical Spirituality

How to Bring More Passion, Creativity and Balance into Everyday Life

Create an intimate relationship with Spirit. This commonsense guide offers practical steps for staying in tune with Spirit midst the hustle and bustle of everyday life. Learn keys, gleaned from the ancient wisdom of the world's spiritual traditions, that show how to discover the soul's core passion, create a sacred space, and use every encounter and circumstance as an opportunity to grow.

112 pp • ISBN 978-0-922729-36-4

Access the Power of Your Higher Self

Your Source of Inner Guidance
and Spiritual Transformation

Access the Power of Your Higher Self presents simple techniques that can help you develop a close, working relationship with Spirit—and experience the joy, peace and empowerment that are your spiritual birthright. When you are in tune with your Higher Self, you become more loving and sensitive to your own and others' needs. You fulfill your life's purpose and express your greatest creativity. Learn ten dynamic steps to spiritual awakening that will help you realize your full potential.

136 pp • ISBN 978-1-932890-11-2

The Story of Your Soul

Recovering the Pearl of Your True Identity

The soul has been likened by some to a pearl that has been cast into the sea of the material universe. The goal of our life is to go after that pearl and recover our true identity. In *The Story of Your Soul,* Elizabeth Clare Prophet tells the story of your soul. It is a story of awakening and overcoming, a story that champions your profound worth and nobility. Includes seven keys for your soul's journey with personal stories, affirmations, meditations and visualizations.

112 pp • ISBN 978-0-922729-42-5

The Creative Power of Sound

Affirmations to Create, Heal and Transform

Recent scientific advances point to what mystics have known for thousands of years: sound holds the key to the creation of the universe—and it can create spiritual and material change in our lives. Prayer is the sound and language of the soul. When spoken out loud, it can unlock the dynamic energy of the spirit. In *The Creative Power of Sound,* you will learn seven principles for applying prayers, mantras and affirmations to your everyday life. You will discover an effective way to harness spiritual energy to create positive change for yourself and the world around you.

ABOUT THE SUMMIT LIGHTHOUSE

Are you interested in the exploration of reality, pursuing individual self-mastery, and finding those points shared in common with the mystical paths of the world's religions? The Summit Lighthouse, an endeavor of the great brotherhood of light, is an international community of spiritual students who share your interest. We publish the teachings of the ascended masters in 30 languages and study them to accelerate on our spiritual path.

What are these teachings? Over the last 150 years, the ascended masters have again brought to mankind's attention the spiritual concepts of the ascension, karma and reincarnation, how to balance one's karma with the violet flame, finding one's twin flame and soul mates to accelerate fulfilling one's divine plan, soul liberation through the power of the spoken Word, prayer and meditation, and finding your point of identity with the reality of your I AM Presence—the divine spark within. Plus information on the long-rumored brotherhood of light that appears in times of need to help mankind.

What is this brotherhood of light? The Great White Brotherhood is comprised of men and women who mastered the fire of the heart, balanced their karma, fulfilled their dharma, and ascended into the light of the presence of God. They return to help souls like you and me, their friends in past lives, to move beyond what we are used to and into that which we really are.

The Summit Lighthouse has its international headquarters at the Royal Teton Ranch, a beautiful land in the Rockies just north of Yellowstone National Park. If you are in the area, we welcome you to drop by for a chat and enjoy our new Yellowstone Hot Springs! This beautiful mineral-rich hot springs is located by the picturesque banks of the Yellowstone River.

Explore the free online lessons on karma, chakras, the archangels, and read an astounding story of Sanat Kumara, the Ancient of Days. View our free book offer, or sign-up for our free series of 16 ePearls on *The Chela and the Path* at:

SummitLighthouse.org

While you're there, learn more about the teachings of the ascended masters, the monthly *Pearls of Wisdom* subscription, the spiritual community at the Royal Teton Ranch, weekend seminars, quarterly conferences, summer retreats, the Keepers of the Flame® Fraternity, or the Ascended Master Library and the study center nearest you.

For a free catalog of books, CDs and DVDs published by Summit University Press, go to:

www.SummitUniversityPress.com

The Summit Lighthouse®
63 Summit Way, Gardiner, Montana 59030 USA
Se habla español.
TSLinfo@TSL.org
SummitLighthouse.org
www.ElizabethClareProphet.com
1-800-245-5445 / 406-848-9500

Elizabeth Clare Prophet is a world-renowned author, spiritual teacher, and pioneer in practical spirituality. Her groundbreaking books have been published in more than thirty languages and over three million copies have been sold worldwide.

Among her best-selling titles are *The Human Aura, The Science of the Spoken Word, Your Seven Energy Centers, The Lost Years of Jesus, The Art of Practical Spirituality,* and her successful Pocket Guides to Practical Spirituality series.

CPSIA information can be obtained
at www.ICGtesting.com
Printed in the USA
JSHW010022190621
16059JS00004B/6